Keswick
and the North Lakes

10 WALKS IN BEAUTIFUL PLACES

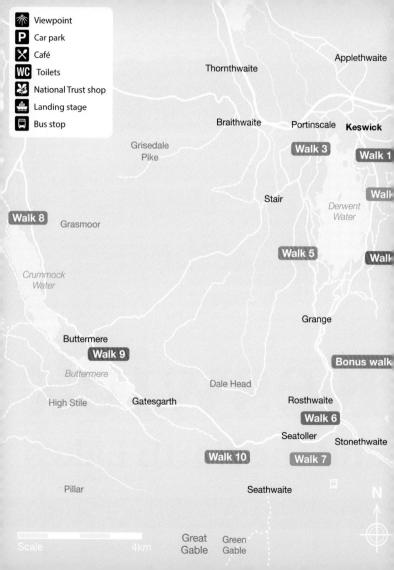

The view from Castlehead in Keswick

Contents

1. Friar's Crag and Castlehead 9

2. Great Wood, Walla Crag and Ashness Bridge 15

3. Derwent Water 21

4. Watendlath to Surprise View 27

5. Cat Bells and Brandelhow Park 31

6. Castle Crag and River Derwent 37

7. Thorneythwaite Farm and Waterfall 43
   Bonus walk Bowder Stone 47

8. Lanthwaite Wood and Crummock Water 49

9. Buttermere 55

10. Honister Pass to Green Gable 59

About the walks

All walks are dog friendly and use Explorer OL4 map.

Easy: Well-maintained, level paths with gentle inclines.
Moderate: Maintained paths that may have tree roots and rocks, with moderate inclines.
Challenging: Rocky terrain, steep inclines or short scrambles.

How to get there

Road: The Borrowdale Road (B5289) starts at Keswick and winds the full length of Borrowdale, along Honister Pass to Buttermere Valley. Most walks start and finish at a National Trust car park. Postcodes in rural locations can cover a wide area – don't trust the SATNAV and do follow road signs. For more information on National Trust car parks in Borrowdale, go to: nationaltrust.org.uk/borrowdale
Bus: Regular bus service 78 from Keswick to Seatoller. Honister Rambler service 77a from Keswick to Honister via Cat Bells

(April–October). Bus services X5 to Keswick from Penrith and Workington, and 555 to Keswick from Lancaster via Ambleside.
Cycle: National Cycle Network 71 passes through Keswick.
Train: Penrith rail station is 18 miles (29km) to the east, with regular trains between Glasgow and London. A regular bus service links Penrith to Keswick.

Walking hints and tips

Hillwalking is an inherently risky activity. The benefits are certainly worth it but you need to keep your wits about you and approach the hills with respect. Here are our top tips for keeping safe on the fells:

➜ Carry an Ordnance Survey map to supplement the maps provided. Take a mobile phone and let someone know where you are going and when you expect to return.
➜ Walk facing oncoming traffic (except at right-hand bends) and wear bright clothing when visibility is poor.

→ An easy to moderate walk can quickly become challenging in adverse weather. Check the forecast and turn back if you don't feel safe – the fell will always be there another day.

→ Take extra care after rain and wear good walking footwear. Natural stone or exposed bedrock can become slippery when wet.

The Countryside Code

Here's how to respect, protect and enjoy the countryside:

✔ Consider the community and always park sensibly, making sure you don't block access to drives, fields or farms.

✔ Leave gates as you find them and follow paths wherever possible, especially where crops are growing.

✔ Leave no trace and take litter home with you.

✔ Avoid damaging, destroying or removing plants and rocks – they are homes to wildlife.

✔ Don't get too close to wild animals or livestock. Keep dogs under control.

Useful numbers

Lake District Search and Mountain Rescue Association
Text where you are and why you need help to 07786 208999.

National Trust for Borrowdale and Buttermere Valley
01768 774649

A natural partnership

We share a love of nature and a passion for the great outdoors with Cotswold Outdoor, so it's natural for us to be working together. Through our partnership, we aim to inspire the nation to explore Britain's incredible coast and countryside on foot – whatever the weather.

In partnership with

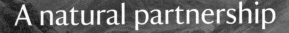

COTSWOLD
outdoor

The outdoor experts at Cotswold Outdoor show us what's inside their kit bag.

Comfy footwear Well-fitting footwear makes a big difference. After all, they are with you every step of the way. Fabric boots are lighter weight, flexible and don't need as much breaking in. Leather is tougher and naturally water resistant, so lasts longer. Also consider what type of terrain you'll be covering; rocky mountain paths will require good ankle support and a deep tread, whereas rambles through grassy fields are better with softer, suppler footwear.

Quality socks However far you roam, good quality socks will keep your feet dry, happy and blister-free. Pick a pair made with natural materials, such as wool – Merino wool is a firm favourite, known for its softness, durability and temperature controlling properties.

A waterproof jacket The famous British weather. We always pack for November in July, just in case. Look for a jacket with taped seams and breathability. High-quality jackets will have a waterproof rating – 10,000mm and above is best for those really stormy days.

A dry bag Keep all your spare layers and electronic devices inside one of these waterproof wonders, stuff it into your rucksack, and shrug off the rain.

Repair tape From patching torn waterproofs to sealing broken zips, this miracle tape has proven itself countless times.

Don't forget, National Trust supporters receive 15% discount at Cotswold Outdoor in store and online.*

* Selected lines are exempt, the discount cannot be used with any other offer or discount and the Partnership discount is only available to National Trust supporters signed up to Cotswold Outdoor's Explore More benefits scheme. Further details of exempt lines and full terms are available here: nationaltrust.org.uk/cotswoldoutdoor. Offer expires on 31.12.21 or as may be extended. Up to 5% of the purchase price paid by National Trust supporters is payable to the National Trust to help look after the places you love to explore. In exceptional circumstances, up to 7% of the purchase price may be payable. The National Trust also receives 50p from each sign up to Explore More by a National Trust supporter.

View across Derwent Water from Friar's Crag

Friar's Crag and Castlehead

Take a lakeside stroll along the foreshore of Derwent Water. This waymarked route takes in two well-known Keswick viewpoints: Friar's Crag and Castlehead.

Starting at the lakeside in Keswick, the route follows the shoreline, pausing at Friar's Crag for an unbroken view across the lake into the 'Jaws of Borrowdale'. You'll pass the Hundred Year Stone to Calfclose Bay – the perfect spot for skimming stones. On the way back, there's an optional hike up to Castlehead for panoramic scenes over Keswick and the surrounding fells.

START/END POINT
National Trust kiosk, Keswick, CA12 5DJ.
Parking at Keswick Lakeside car park (not National Trust).

FACILITIES
Public toilets, cafés and the National Trust snack kiosk at the lakeside.

Viewpoints

Moderate

269ft (82m)

3.4 miles (5.5km)

2 – 2½ hours

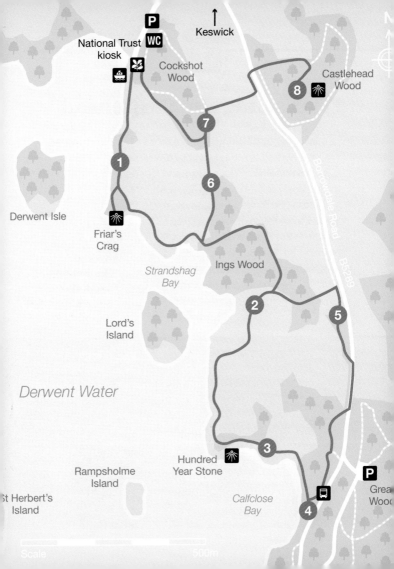

1 | From the National Trust kiosk, follow the road with the lake on your right. At the fork, head right to pause at Friar's Crag, before continuing on the route. Pass through a gate and follow the path round the lakeshore, over a footbridge and into Ings Wood. Go through the wood, following the boardwalk.

2 | Leave the wood through a stone gateway. Turn right onto a wide, surfaced track. Continue over a cattle grid and into a field.

3 | Following the line of the lakeshore, you'll pass the Hundred Year Stone. After a small footbridge, the path becomes less defined on the shingle beach of Calfclose Bay. At the top of the shoreline, the path becomes visible again.

4 | Turn left off the main path into the woods towards the Borrowdale Road. Continue over two footbridges. Leave the woods between a drystone wall and a fence on the path running parallel to the road, until you reach a crossroads.

> 'The first thing I remember is being taken by my nurse to the brow of Friar's Crag.'

John Ruskin

▼ JOHN RUSKIN MEMORIAL
In a grove of trees near Friar's Crag there is a slate memorial to John Ruskin. His writings on the connection between people and the landscape inspired the founders of the National Trust.

5 | Turn left down the track. When you reach a junction, turn right and go back through Ings Wood.

6 | After leaving Ings Wood, instead of continuing onwards to Friar's Crag, turn right across a field. Cross the boardwalk and through a gate into **Cockshot Wood**, bearing right.

7 | **Decision time** | At the crossroads, either turn right to hike up Castlehead or turn left back to the lakeside. For **Castlehead**, follow the path until you reach the Borrowdale Road. Cross the road and into **Castlehead Wood**. The left-hand path curves upwards through the woodland.

Calfclose Bay on the shores of Derwent Water, with Walla Crag rising in the distance. ▶

▼HUNDRED YEAR STONE
Crafted to mark 100 years of the National Trust looking after the Lake District. It's made from Borrowdale volcanic rock and features a single, unbroken line tracing a hundred corners.

8 | As the path levels out, turn right. A few rocky steps lead to a clearing at the top with panoramic views of Keswick and Derwent Water. There's a toposcope naming all the fells in sight. When ready, retrace your steps until the crossroads at **point 7**. Then go straight on to return to the lakeshore and snack kiosk.

▲WILD DERWENT
Derwent Water is home to Britain's rarest freshwater fish – the vendace, a type of freshwater herring. Calfclose Bay is named after the cormorants ('skarv' is the Old Norse word for cormorant), which can often be seen drying their wings on sandbanks out in the lake. Cockshot Wood is named after the woodcock – sometimes seen at dawn or dusk.

End

National Trust kiosk, Keswick, CA12 5DJ

Ancient oak woodland near Ashness Bridge

Great Wood, Walla Crag and Ashness Bridge

Wander through Great Wood, over Walla Crag, and across open moorland to Ashness Bridge – one of the most photographed bridges in the Lake District.

Setting off from the heart of the woodland, the rocky path follows a steep incline into open fields. Due to the amount of rainfall each year, the Borrowdale woodlands classify as temperate rainforests. Take care on the paths, as they can be slippery.

START/END POINT
Great Wood National Trust car park, CA12 5UP.
Note: the location of the car park differs from the OS map, which is incorrect.

FACILITIES
The Bark House hut is often open in the summer for a cuppa and chat with the volunteers (opening times dependent on volunteer availability).

Woodland

Moderate

915ft
(279m)

4.5 miles
(7.2km)

2 hours

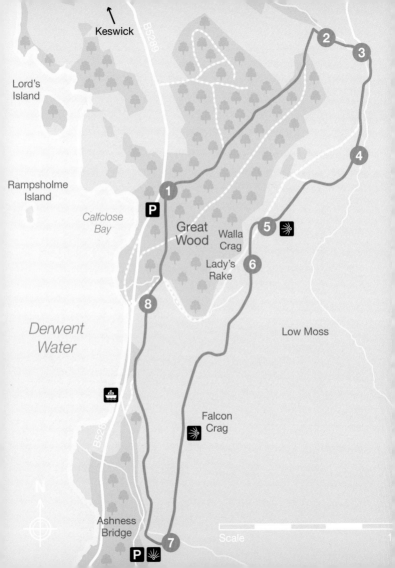

Keswick

Lord's
Island

Rampsholme
Island

Calfclose
Bay

Great
Wood

Walla
Crag

Lady's
Rake

Low Moss

Derwent
Water

Falcon
Crag

Ashness
Bridge

Scale

N

1
2
3
4
5
6
7
8

1 | With the main road behind you, and Walla Crag rising up ahead, take the small path in the top-left corner of the car park. Continue for ½ mile (0.8km), rising steadily through the woods. After crossing a couple of small streams, the woods give way to fields on the left and views over Keswick to Bassenthwaite Lake and Skiddaw.

2 | At the T-junction, turn right signposted to Castlerigg and Walla Crag. Follow the path with the deep valley of Brockle Beck to the left.

3 | Crossing the beck at the wooden footbridge, follow the track up to the gate and turn right along the tarmac lane. At the fork below Rakefoot Farm, bear right towards another footbridge, re-crossing the beck. The route becomes a stony track rising through a gate, towards more open ground, with a wall to your right.

WALLA CRAG

Walla Crag is part of a series of volcanic rocks that form the rugged scenery of the 'Jaws of Borrowdale'. On a clear day, you can see beyond Bassenthwaite Lake to the Solway Firth and hills of Galloway in Scotland.

LADY'S RAKE

Below Walla Crag is Lady's Rake, a narrow cleft in the face of the crag. The Countess of Derwent Water allegedly took this perilous route when fleeing from Lord's Island (one of the seven islands on Derwent Water) after the capture of her husband during the Jacobite Rebellion of 1745.

Crag – a protruding piece of rugged rock or cliff face.

▶ASHNESS BRIDGE

Ashness Bridge is a traditional packhorse bridge. The parapets are deliberately low so that heavily laden packhorses – the main form of transport in the fells for hundreds of years – could cross the bridge without their packs getting stuck.

▼THE ATLANTIC OAKWOODS OF BORROWDALE

The oak woodlands in Borrowdale have one of the most important assemblages of mosses, lichens, ferns and liverworts in northern Europe.

4 | At the end of the wall, take the greener track straight ahead, keeping alongside Brockle Beck rather than the eroded path that goes off alongside the wall to the right. Follow this green track towards an isolated tree on the skyline. Then bear left towards the summit of Walla Crag as it comes into view.

5 | Cross the wall at the stile. Bear left towards the pile of stones and the summit. A rocky platform ahead opens up stunning views. With the lake behind you, continue along the path until it re-crosses the wall at the next stile.

6 | Take the track to the left which arcs across the moorland, avoiding the steep descent into Cat Gill. After crossing the head of the streams, bear right until you see the track leading to the white buildings of Ashness Farm in the distance.

7 | Turn right before the footbridge and follow the river down to Ashness Bridge. After taking some photos, walk down the road a few metres then follow the footpath signposted to Great Wood. After the first gate, keep to the lower path on the left.

8 | As you approach Great Wood, the path rises at a wall to cross a footbridge over the base of Cat Gill. Continue back down to the car park. A path across the road from the car park leads to Calfclose Bay and the lakeshore path to Keswick, a further 1.5 miles (2.5km) away.

▲A FALCON'S VIEW
As you walk back to Great Wood from Ashness Bridge, listen out for the sharp cry of peregrine falcons. Falcon Crag towers above the path and it's a good place to listen for their calls and watch for their distinctive 'hunched-shoulder' silhouette.

End

Great Wood National Trust car park,
CA12 5UP

A jetty on Derwent Water

Derwent Water

Take a whole day to enjoy this gentle walk around the entirety of Derwent Water, the 'Queen of the Lakes'.

The route starts at the National Trust kiosk in Keswick and heads clockwise around the lakeshore, with a short section on road. If you need to shorten the trip, there are several landing stages along the way where you can catch a boat back to Keswick.

START/END POINT
National Trust kiosk, Keswick, CA12 5DJ.
Parking at Keswick Lakeside car park (not National Trust).

FACILITIES
Public toilets, cafés and the National Trust snack kiosk at the lakeside in Keswick.

Lakeside

Moderate

Level walk

10 miles (16km)

5 hours

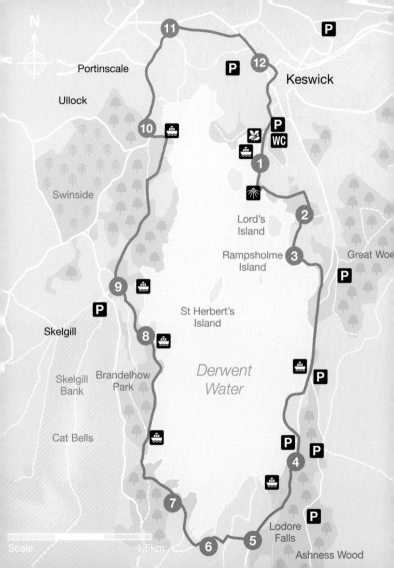

1 | From the Keswick National Trust shop, follow the road with the lake on your right. At the fork, go right to Friar's Crag before re-joining the path, through two gates and into Ings Wood.

2 | Leave the wood and turn right along a wide track. Cross a cattle grid through a field and past Stable Hills cottages. Keeping the lake on your right, continue into a small wood. Enjoy the views from the Millennium Seat, before continuing onwards to reach Calfclose Bay and the Hundred Year Stone.

3 | From Calfclose Bay, continue over a wooden footbridge, following the path left beside the ghyll and over a stile, past Ashness Gate, until you reach Kettlewell car park (NT) and landing stage.

▲BEATRIX POTTER'S KESWICK
Between 1885 and 1907, Beatrix Potter spent many summers on the shores of Derwent Water. It was during this time she created the beloved tales of Squirrel Nutkin, Benjamin Bunny and Mrs. Tiggy-Winkle. Many recognisable views feature in her sketches.

▲LAND OF THE LAKES

After the Ice Ages, Derwent Water and Bassenthwaite formed one lake. Silt, carried down into the lake by the River Greta from the east and Newlands Beck from the west, gradually created marshes that separated the lakes. They became one again during the floods of 2005 and 2009. The settlements are mainly on little rounded hills in the lowlands, such as those that form the islands in the lake.

LODORE FALLS

It was the private sale of Lodore Falls in the 1890s that galvanised local vicar Hardwicke Rawnsley to co-found the National Trust to ensure beautiful places could remain open to everyone.

Ghyll – a northern term for a deep ravine or narrow mountain stream. The word originates from the Old Norse 'gil'.

4 | At Kettlewell car park, the route leaves the shoreline and goes through SSSI woodland. Exit the car park, cross the road and turn right along a footpath adjacent to the road, separated by a stone wall, signposted Lodore Falls.

5 | At the fork near Lodore Hotel, bear right onto the road. Walk past the hotel until you reach a gate and stile on the right, leading to a broad track signposted to Manesty. Follow the track to the River Derwent and another footbridge into marsh meadowland.

Diversion (2 miles) | In case of high water levels, continue along the road to Grange and over a road bridge, where a waymarked track leads you back to lakeshore.

6 | Go through the gate at the far end of the boardwalk. Continue along a gravelled path, keeping the lake on your right.

7 | Enter the woodland through a gate and continue through the trees to a drive. Turn right and bear left uphill to a kissing gate, passing the mine workings of Brandelhow Bay. Keep to the shoreline to High Brandelhow Jetty. Continue on the path, keeping the lake on your right, through the woodlands of Brandelhow Park. Look out for the hands sculpture (see page 34).

8 | Where the path forks, turn left away from the lake. After another gate, the path bears right to a tarmac drive. Turn right, past the Hawes End Outdoor Centre.

9 | Take the second path on your right, just past the private drive to Derwent Bay, descending through woodland, across a field, into more woodland. Go through a gate, cross a road, and follow the waymarked track. Cross a drive and descend the path to Nichol End Marine and landing stage.

10 | Turn left and continue to Portinscale village. Turn right and walk through the village. At the road junction, turn right on the waymarked path past Derwent Water Hotel and over the suspension bridge.

11 | Continue on the road for 328ft (100m). Turn right onto a footpath between two fields. At the main road, cross the bridge over the River Greta and continue on to Keswick.

12 | To return to the start, go through the Market Square, past Moot Hall, and down Lake Road. Follow signs to the lake and Hope Park Gardens.

End

National Trust kiosk, Keswick, CA12 5DJ

Watendlath Beck in autumn

Watendlath to Surprise View

A riverside walk to one of Derwent Water's most celebrated viewpoints: Surprise View.

This out-and-back route starts at the charming hamlet of Watendlath, with its traditional packhorse bridge and tranquil tarn. The stone-pitched path follows the Watendlath Beck, flanked by valley hills, and into the canopy of Ashness Wood. It's a level walk but can be rocky in places.

START/END POINT
Watendlath National Trust car park, CA12 5UW.

FACILITIES
Café (not National Trust) and public toilets at Watendlath.

Riverside

Easy

Level walk

5 miles (8km)

3 hours

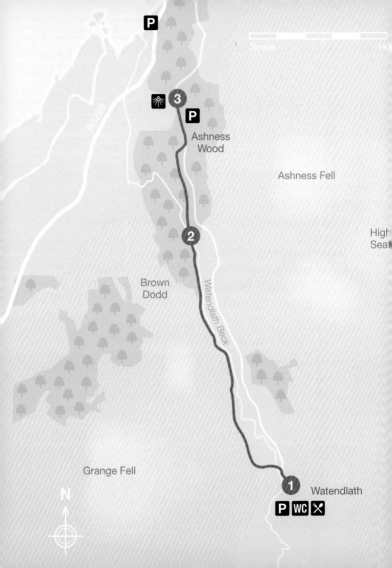

Scale

1km

P

3

P

Ashness
Wood

Ashness Fell

B5289

Brown
Dodd

Waterdlath Beck

High
Sea

Grange Fell

1

Watendlath

P WC X

N

1 | Starting at Watendlath, cross the packhorse bridge over the river. Turn right, with the tarn behind you, and take the footpath alongside Watendlath Beck. Keeping the river on your right, follow the stone-pitched path all the way to the wooden footbridge at Moss Mine.

2 | Cross the footbridge and turn left through a gate. Follow the footpath gently uphill and through Ashness Wood. Keep on the footpath until it meets the road.

3 | Walk down the road a few metres and you'll soon arrive at Surprise View. It's the end of a hanging valley; the main Borrowdale glacier sliced through the side valley, creating a heady vertical drop and glorious views over Derwent Water towards Keswick. When ready, retrace your steps to Watendlath.

End
Watendlath National Trust car park,
CA12 5UW

WATENDLATH TALES

The secluded hamlet of Watendlath was the home of Judith Paris in Hugh Walpole's fictional *Rogue Herries* chronicles, set in 18th-century Borrowdale.

▼ANCIENT ASHES

There are over 100 ash pollard trees at Watendlath. This traditional way of cropping branches from trees to provide tools, firewood and fodder for livestock has prolonged the lives of these ancient trees. Some of them may be almost 1,000 years old.

Cat Bells in autumn

Cat Bells and Brandelhow Park

A mountain in miniature. At 1,480ft (451m) high, Cat Bells is a popular, family-friendly fell with classic Lake District mountain terrain.

This circular walk starts at Hawes End Jetty on the quiet side of Derwent Water. It finishes with a lakeside amble through the peaceful park at Brandelhow – the birthplace of the National Trust in the Lakes. There are no facilities nearby, so make sure to pack a picnic.

START/END POINT

Hawes End Jetty, nr Portinscale, Keswick. Nearest postcode CA12 5UB.

FACILITIES

There is limited parking at Cat Bells. We recommend you arrive by boat, bus or cycle from Keswick.

Low fell	Challenging	1,187ft (361m)	3.5 miles (5.5km)	3 hours

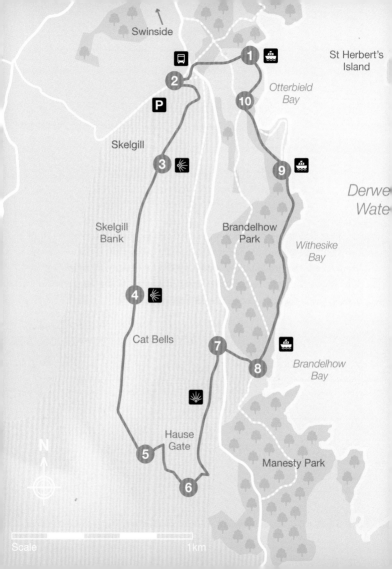

1 | From Hawes End Jetty, take the footpath signposted 'Cat Bells ½ mile' to the base of the fell. Go through a gate to meet the road and head right. At the cattle grid, go through another gate to a road junction with Skelgill signposted from its apex.

2 | Cross the road and take the stone-pitched footpath signposted 'Cat Bells 1 mile'. Climb the path as it bends round the nose of the ridge. The rule is: if it's going up, it's the right way. It's steep at first, but will ease off eventually.

3 | Get ready to *scramble!* This is the first 'rock step' or short scramble section – a practice for the summit. If you're unfamiliar with scrambling, the key is to keep three points of contact at all times – either two hands and one foot, or two feet and one hand. Once at the top, the

'I have seen that door into the back of the hill called Cat Bells – and besides, I am very well acquainted with dear Mrs. Tiggy-Winkle!'

Beatrix Potter,
The Tale of Mrs. Tiggy-Winkle (1905)

▼LAIR OF THE WILD CAT
Cat Bells derives from 'Cat Bields', meaning shelter of the wild cat. Possibly named when wild cats used to roam these parts centuries ago. We've created stone-pitched paths to protect the fragile mountain soils. Please help us protect the fells from erosion by keeping to the ridgeline and avoiding the side slopes.

▲THE HANDS SCULPTURE
This sculpture is called *Entrust*. It was carved from a fallen oak tree by sculptor John Merrill to mark the 100th anniversary of Brandelhow Park opening to the public.

BRANDELHOW PARK
In 1902, Brandelhow became the first place in the Lake District to be protected for the nation by the National Trust. Its role in the history of a global conservation movement is one of the reasons why the Lake District became a World Heritage Site in 2017.

slope eases off. This can feel like a false summit – look up and you'll see the real summit ahead.

4 | Start the final scramble to the top of Cat Bells. Take your time, move carefully and enjoy the panoramic views at the top. When ready, go down the other side of the fell on a gradual slope to the col at Hause Gate.

5 | At Hause Gate, there's an indistinct crossroads at the col. Take the left-hand stone-pitched path down towards the lake to meet the Cat Bells terrace path.

6 | At the junction near the stone wall, turn left towards the Cat Bells terrace path, signposted to the lake and Hawes End Jetty. Follow the path until it dips down to meet the road.

7 | **Decision time** | either continue on this path to the cattle grid at point 2, or go down to the lakeside and through Brandelhow Park back to Hawes End Jetty. To walk along the lakeside, cross the road and take the footpath signposted 'To the Lake/High Brandelhow Jetty ¼ mile' downhill.

8 | At the bottom of the hill, go through a wooden gate into the woodland. Follow the path left along the lakeside to Low Brandelhow Jetty. From here, you can catch the boat to Keswick or

continue along the lakeside back to Hawes End Jetty. Following the path with the lake on your left, you'll pass the sculpture of the hands.

9 | Where the path forks, go left (the right takes you on a short loop along the edge of woods and back to the main path).

10 | Keep on the main path until another fork. This time, turn right off the main path and towards the lake signposted to Hawes End Jetty.

▲ **BRANDELHOW WILDLIFE**
On the quiet side of Derwent Water, away from roads, Brandelhow Park is rich in wildlife. It's home to kingfishers, woodpeckers, nuthatches, roe deer and red squirrels.

Hause – *the Cumbrian name for col or pass, the low point between two peaks.*

End

Hawes End Jetty, nr Portinscale, Keswick.
Nearest postcode CA12 5UB

Looking over Derwent Water to Skiddaw from the top of Castle Crag

Castle Crag and River Derwent

The civilised way to climb Castle Crag. Known as the 'smallest Wainwright', the hilltop affords views over Borrowdale and Buttermere valley.

This scenic route starts with a short climb from Seatoller hamlet and follows a rolling contour route, with glorious views down the valley. After reaching the top of Castle Crag, the rocky path circles back along the banks of the River Derwent.

START/END POINT	**FACILITIES**
Seatoller National Trust car park, CA12 5XN.	Public toilets at Seatoller car park. Refreshments for walkers at the YHA hostel and the Flock Inn pub, run by our tenant farmers.

Riverside

Moderate

590ft (180m)

5 miles (8km)

3½ – 4 hours

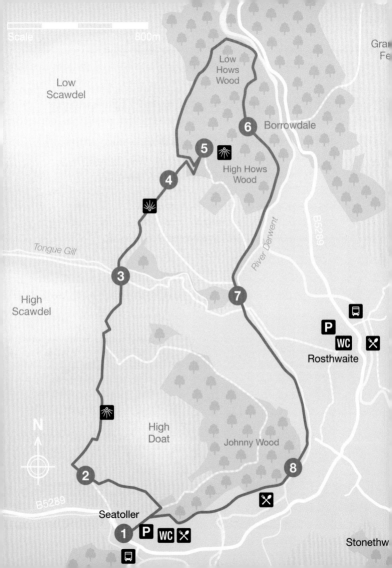

1 | Leave Seatoller car park through the gate signposted to Johnny Wood. Follow the track and take the left-hand fork. At the stream, turn left, climbing towards a line of four Scots pine trees. At the trees, turn right to join the main track. Follow the track as it curves left through a gate. Carry on through two more gates to where the path crosses another stream.

2 | At the stream, turn hard right and walk uphill to a gate. Go through the gate and turn right along the wall. You have now joined the old mine road that was used for Honister slate mine. This track goes all the way to Castle Crag.

3 | The footbridge across Tongue Gill is a key landmark on the way – and the biggest gill the path crosses before Castle Crag. Continue along the track and at the cusp of the brow you will get your first glimpse of Derwent Water.

4 | Just over the brow, there's a 'sheep track' path to the right, which avoids losing height. This path skirts round the base of a crag and follows the fence to a ladder stile. Climb the stile and

WAR MEMORIAL MOUNTAIN

After the First World War, the family of 2nd Lieutenant John Hamer donated Castle Crag to the National Trust. The memorial in his memory is dedicated to 'the men of Borrowdale' who lost their lives in the war.

▼G&T ANYONE?

Juniper bushes can be seen growing in the crags. Up here, the terrain is too steep for Herdwick sheep, so the saplings don't get grazed off. The scrub also provides vital habitat for many rare native upland birds and insects.

turn right to join the main path to the top of **Castle Crag**.

5 | Take in the views from the top. When ready, retrace your steps down the crag but don't go back over the ladder stile. Instead, follow the main path down the hill. Once in the woods, take the right hand fork over the footbridge. On reaching the **River Derwent**, follow the path signposted 'Rosthwaite 1¾ miles'. You're now on the return leg of the walk.

6 | There is a fork in the path heading up to the right, signposted to **Millican Dalton's Cave**. Take a short detour to the cave, returning to this point, before continuing straight on towards Rosthwaite.

7 | Go past the packhorse bridge (this will take

◄MILLICAN DALTON'S CAVE

Each summer for nearly 50 years, the 'professor of adventure' would retreat to what is now known as Dalton's Cave. Millican Dalton made his living as a mountain guide and sailed his homemade raft into Keswick for coffee and cigarettes. His words are carved into the wall of the upper cave: 'Don't waste words, jump to conclusions.'

you to Rosthwaite for buses back to Seatoller). Continue straight on and over the footbridge. Keeping on the path beside the river, go past the stepping-stones until you get to the YHA hostel at **Longthwaite** – a great pit stop for walkers.

8 | From the hostel, follow the path along the river back to **Seatoller**. There's a short scramble section with a chain attached to the rock to help you – take it steady and it's less daunting than it looks. The path then goes round the bottom of **Johnny Wood**, along the wall and back to the car park.

▲RIVERLANDS

Rivers need the ability to meander naturally in order to stay healthy. They also need gravels for fish to spawn and clean water that supports insect and bird life. The River Derwent is part of the National Trust's £10 million Riverlands project, which aims to bring UK rivers back to life following years of repeat flooding and damage to habitats and local communities.

End

Seatoller National Trust car park,
CA12 5XN

Thorneythwaite Farm in the heart of Borrowdale

Thorneythwaite Farm and Waterfall

This picturesque walk introduces you to three parts of Thorneythwaite hill farm: the in-bye land, the intake land and the open fell.

Starting at Seatoller, this out-and-back route passes through hay meadows and wood pasture as they undergo gradual restoration. It then continues through the fell wall to a hidden valley and finishes at a picnic spot beside a waterfall.

START/END POINT	FACILITIES
National Trust Seatoller car park. Bus stop outside car park, CA12 5XN.	Public toilets at Seatoller car park. There's also a craft shop at Seatoller Farm run by our tenant farmers.

Waterfall

Moderate

492ft (150m)

2.3 miles (3.6 km)

1 hour 10 mins

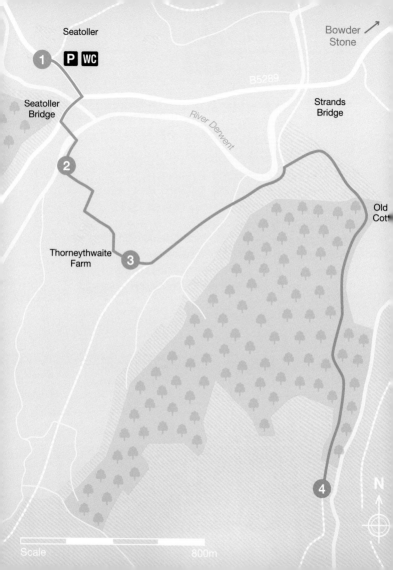

Seatoller

P **WC**

Bowder
Stone

Seatoller
Bridge

B5289

Strands
Bridge

River Derwent

Old
Cott

Thorneythwaite
Farm

1

2

3

4

N

Scale

800m

Start

National Trust Seatoller car park.
Bus stop outside car park,
CA12 5XN

1 | From Seatoller car park, go left down the road. At the junction, turn right onto the road signposted 'Seathwaite 1 mile'. Go through the first wooden gate on the left onto a public footpath (note: there are yurts in the field April–October).

▼HAY MEADOW RESTORATION

Since the 1970s, 90% of England's hay meadows have been lost due to intensive farming. Thorneythwaite's fields are being restored to nature-rich hay meadows by avoiding fertilisers and cutting the grass later in the season, allowing wildflowers to naturally re-pollinate the fields over the next 10 years.

▲WILD APPLES

Thorneythwaite's wood pasture is unique due to its abundance of wild apple trees. Since sheep were introduced they have nibbled down the young tree saplings. Today, it is once again grazed by cattle that don't damage the saplings.

RARE LICHENS

The trees in the wood pasture are host to some very rare 'old growth forest lichens'. These species grew in forests that sprang up when the glaciers receded nearly 10,000 years ago and they're still hanging on (just!). They're very sensitive to fertilisers, which is another reason why we're adopting more nature-friendly farming techniques.

2 | Cross the footbridge, turn right and follow the edges of the field. Turn right again into the next field and follow the wall to a gap on the left. Go through two gates to join the tarmacked lane.

3 | Turn left and walk along the lane away from the farmhouse. Following it left round a corner, continue between the walls for 1/3 mile (500m). Turn right onto a public footpath signposted to Glaramara. Go through the gate and walk up a rough track as it winds up the hill and through the next two gates.

4 | Go through the gate in the fell wall and onto the open fell. Follow the path as it climbs until you reach a large waterfall on the left. Find a picnic spot and enjoy the sound of rushing water – just watch out for the steep drops. When ready, retrace your steps back to the car park.

End

National Trust Seatoller car park, CA12 5XN

◄HERDWICK SHEEP

There are no fell walls between here and the farms in Langdale. It's still farmland, but the Herdwick sheep don't need walls; they know where to go and will only stray if pushed by bad weather. The lambs are called 'hoggs' after their first winter, and Herdwick 'hoggett' is available from February. Many local restaurants have it on the menu for its deep, rich flavour. By sampling hogget you're supporting the local economy, enabling farmers to manage the land for nature.

BONUS WALK

Bowder Stone (½ mile/40 mins)

From the National Trust Bowder Stone car park CA12 5XA, go down to the road and follow signposts for ¼ mile to the Bowder Stone.

►BOWDER STONE

It has been beguiling travellers to the Lake District for centuries. The Bowder Stone is six times the height of a person and is improbably balanced on one edge. In 2019 a ladder was installed, reminiscent of the original 'crazy ladder' used by thrill-seeking Georgian tourists.

View of Crummock Water and Brackenthwaite Hows

Lanthwaite Wood and Crummock Water

One walk, two spectacular views. Look over the famous vista of the Buttermere fells from across Crummock Water, as well as the dramatic, rocky buttress of Grasmoor End that looms over the northern end of the lake.

From Crummock Water car park near the hamlet of Loweswater, you'll walk through woodland and along the lakeshore. On the way back, there's an optional hike up to the vista at Brackenthwaite Hows – a popular spot with Georgian and Victorian travellers.

START/END POINT	FACILITIES
Crummock Water National Trust car park, CA13 0RT.	The hamlet of Loweswater is half a mile away and is home to the Kirkstile Inn pub.

Viewpoints

Moderate

208m (682ft)

4 miles (6.4 km)

2½ hours

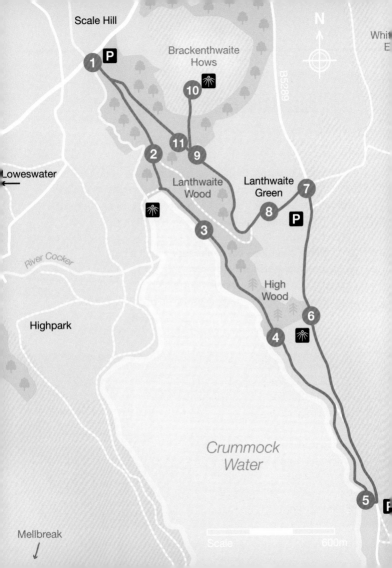

1 | Leave the car park through the wooden gate. Follow the forest road straight on, ignoring the left-hand fork. Walk through the forest with stolen glimpses of the meandering River Cocker below.

2 | Stay on the main track, ignoring the left-hand forks, down to the lake. From the lakeshore, take the narrow 'trod' uphill through the trees. Turn right and follow the track as it gently climbs. On the right are views of the lake across to Mellbreak.

3 | At the junction, turn right down towards the boathouse – a great spot for a picnic and a paddle. Then follow the path that continues into the wood along the lake edge. Go through a gate and over a ford and a stile. Here the path gets rough under foot.

4 | At the end of High Wood, pass through a gate and follow the path ahead. Stay on this path as it hugs the lakeshore, passing through two gates and over three footbridges, until you come to a wall with no gate.

▼ Walk through tranquil woodlands that hug the lakeshore.

EARLY INDUSTRY
The now peaceful shores of Crummock Water were once home to early industry. On this route, you'll pass the site of one kiln, now under a bench, and a bloomery site – the earliest form of iron production. Look for fragments of waste iron slag among the rocks on the beach (but please leave them here).

5 | On reaching the wall, turn left and walk uphill to arrive at a gate. Don't go through the gate – instead, turn left and follow the grassy path keeping the boundary wall on your right, heading back the way you came. Keep right at the junction, taking the higher path running adjacent to the wall. This path gives lovely views across Crummock Water.

6 | Arrive at the edge of High Wood – a bench marks the spot where artist J.M.W Turner made his sketches of the valley. Pass through the gate onto the road. Turn left and follow the roadside verge, keeping the wood to your left. Take care as the verge narrows in places.

7 | Immediately after **Lanthwaite Green**, turn left over the stone stile marked by the public footpath finger post. Follow the track as it runs between the boundaries.

8 | Where a wall crosses the track, pass through the kissing gate on the left. A slate footpath sign helps guide the way. Walk towards the wood ahead and through another gate. Go through the gate and follow the path that hugs the boundary wall to the next gate.

9 | **Decision time** | Either turn left onto the main path as it heads downhill back to the car park, or you can do an optional hike to see the viewing station at

◄ View of Crummock Water from the lakeside.

Brackenthwaite Hows. For Brackenthwaite Hows, at the gate keep straight on keeping the boundary wall on your right – the path narrows and winds uphill through trees to a narrow gate in the boundary wall.

10 | Go through the gate out of the wood and keep following the narrow path uphill to a low summit. This is Brackenthwaite Hows. Enjoy the view then retrace your steps.

11 | Follow the path downhill, ignoring forks to the left and right, until it re-joins the main forestry road leading back to the car park.

End

Crummock Water National Trust car park, CA13 0RT

LOOKING AFTER THE LAKES

Crummock Water is one of few lakes that is free from New Zealand Pygmyweed, an invasive species that's taken over Derwent Water and Bassenthwaite. Please help us prevent this weed from getting into Crummock Water by checking your boots, wetsuits and pets.

INSPIRATIONAL VIEWS

The view from Brackenthwaite Hows was a fixture for Victorian tourists. It was mentioned in an 1879 guide as 'The Station', a viewpoint attached to the old Scale Hill Hotel. The view from the lakeshore is also a classic. It was this view that was sketched by artist J.M.W Turner on his first visit to the Lake District. It inspired his watercolour painting *Crummock Water Looking Towards Buttermere*.

Buttermere Lake seen from Fleetwith Pike

Buttermere

Feel right in the heart of the fells with this gentle
walk around the tranquil waters of Buttermere.
It's one of the best round-the-lake walks the
Lake District has to offer.

Start and finish in Buttermere village with its cosy pubs for
weary walkers. Perfect for families, it can get busy
in the high season, so arrive early for a more
peaceful experience.

START/END POINT	FACILITIES
Buttermere National Trust car park, CA13 9UZ (¼ mile outside the village towards Cockermouth).	There are two pubs in Buttermere village: the Fish Inn and the Bridge Hotel. There's also a small tea rooms (summer opening only).

Lakeside

Easy

Level walk

4.5 miles
(7.5km)

1½ hours

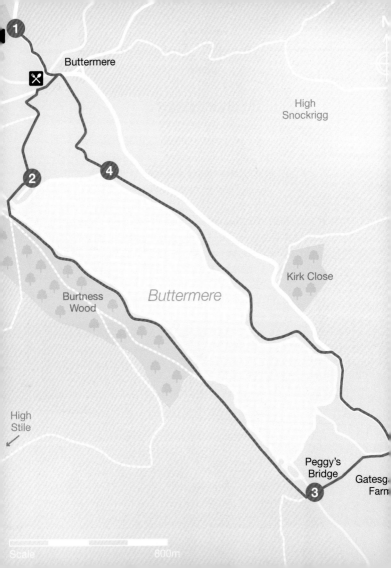

Buttermere

High
Snockrigg

Kirk Close

Buttermere

Burtness
Wood

High
Stile

Peggy's
Bridge

Gatesg
Farm

Scale   800m

Start

1 | Turn right out of the car park and follow the road to the village. At the Bridge Hotel, turn right, taking the track to the left of the Fish Inn pub. Follow this path until you reach the lakeside.

2 | At the lakeside, turn right and cross over a footbridge into the woodland. Keeping the water on your left, follow the path down the lake.

3 | Turn left over Peggy's Bridge to reach Gatesgarth Farm. At the farm, turn left again and head back towards the lake, walking 1/3 mile (600m) on the road. On reaching the lake, carry on through a tunnel and back towards Buttermere village.

4 | Where the path forks, carry straight on to the village and back to the car park.

A TALE OF TWO LAKES

After the last Ice Age, Buttermere and Crummock Water were one lake. Over time, the natural erosion of the fells caused loose material from the mountains to flow down the becks and form the spit of land where Buttermere village now sits.

BENEATH THE WATERS

The deep, chilly, crystal-clear waters of both lakes make ideal conditions for Arctic Charr fish, stranded here at the end of the Ice Age. Brown trout, sea trout and salmon are also regular inhabitants. Below the surface, divers see freshwater sponges attached to the cliffs. In sheltered bays, the lilac flowers of water lobelia emerge from their long stems.

End

Buttermere National Trust car park,
CA13 9UZ

View down into Ennerdale Valley

Honister Pass to Green Gable

Experience the wilderness of the high fells with this
out-and-back route to the top of Green Gable –
one of 14 Cumbrian peaks gifted to the National Trust
after the First World War.

The route starts at the heady heights of Honister Pass.
After a short, steep climb, the trail follows a gradual
incline with grand valley views all the way to the top of
Green Gable. Best on a clear day, so do check the
forecast before setting out.

START/END POINT
National Trust Honister car park,
CA12 5XN.
Situated 350m (1,148ft) high along
the Honister Pass road.

FACILITIES
Café and toilets at Honister Slate
Mine (not National Trust).

High fells

Challenging

**1,476ft
(450m)**

**2.5 miles
(4 km)**

3 – 4 hours

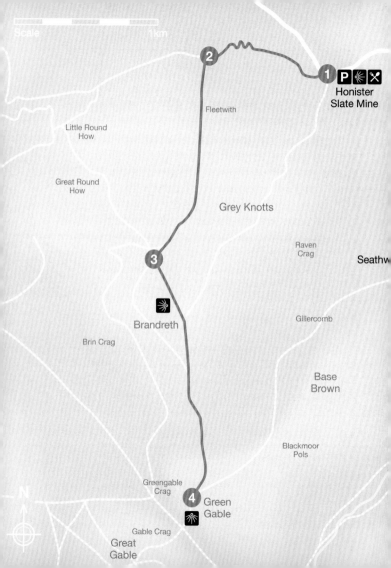

Scale

1km

②

① P ☀ ✕
Honister
Slate Mine

Fleetwith

Little Round
How

Great Round
How

Grey Knotts

Raven
Crag

Seathw

③

☀

Brandreth

Gillercomb

Brin Crag

Base
Brown

Blackmoor
Pols

Greengable
Crag

④ Green
Gable
☀

N

Gable Crag

Great
Gable

1 | Before setting off, pause to look over Borrowdale from the edge of the car park. Then go through the wooden gate in the far corner, past the Honister Slate Mine visitor entrance and into the mine car park. Take the stone-pitched path signposted 'Gatesgarth via Dubs 2½ mile'. Ascend the steep climb for 2/3 mile (1 km).

2 | At the raised stone platform, turn left off the main path onto a grassy path. Follow this footpath as it gently climbs, using the cairns to guide you. Rising above to the left is Grey Knotts. On the right, the view down to Buttermere Valley is gradually revealed. On a clear day, three lakes are visible: Buttermere, then Crummock Water, with Loweswater glimpsed in the distance.

▲ *Cairn* – *a man-made pile of stones. Usually found on summits and viewpoints, they act as waymarkers in the high fells.*

SLATE MINING

Until the mid-20th century, quarrying was the traditional employment of many local people. Slate was loaded onto wooden sledges and then sledged downhill with the quarrymen running ahead.

THE GREAT GIFT

Green Gable is one of 14 Lake District summits that were dedicated as war memorials after the First World War. At the time, it was the biggest gift of open countryside to the National Trust.

3 | Continue to climb as the path bends round and uphill to the left. Head towards the stile in the wire fence. Go over the stile and continue on the path, down past a tarn, before climbing the final stretch to the summit of Green Gable.

HYDRO POWER AT HONISTER

You might think that the wettest spot in England would be a good place for generating renewable energy – and you'd be right. Just below Honister at Hause Gill is a green energy hydro power scheme. It generated almost 10,000 kWh in its first week – the equivalent of 10,000 dishwasher cycles. And the best bit? You wouldn't even know it was there.

◄ Looking towards Great Gable from Green Gable.

4 | At the top, enjoy views over the valleys with Great Gable towering ahead of you. Then retrace your steps back to Honister Slate Mine visitor centre and café for some well-earned tea and cake.

End

National Trust Honister car park,
CA12 5XN

First published in the United Kingdom in 2021 by
Pitkin Publishing
An imprint of Pavilion Books Ltd.
43 Great Ormond Street
London
WC1N 3HZ

Copyright © National Trust 2021

Text by Emily Roe with thanks the National Trust North Lakes team.

Picture credits: © National Trust Images: NTI/Paul Harris: 1, 5, 13 (left), 36, 51, 54, 62–63; NTI/Emily Roe: 3, 61; NTI/John Malley: 6, 18 (left and right), 26, 30, 35, 39, 41, 42, 45, 47 (top), 48, 52–53, 58; NTI/Natasha Balletta: 8; NTI/Joe Cornish: 11, 20, 34; NTI/Val Corbett: 12; NTI/Zoe Frank: 13 (right); NTI/Michael Hirst: 14; NTI/Nick Upton: 19; NTI/Robert Thrift: 23; NTI/Chris Lacey: 24, 47 (bottom); NTI/David Sellman: 29; NTI/John Millar: 33; NTI/John Miller: 46.

Front cover: NTI/Joe Cornish. Back cover (top and bottom): NTI/Paul Harris. Front flap 1: NTI/Natasha Balletta; 2: NTI/Michael Hirst; 3: NTI/Joe Cornish; 4, 5, 7, 8, 10: NTI/John Malley; 6, 9: NTI/Paul Harris. Back flap: NTI/Paul Harris.

All maps by Sudden Impact Media Ltd.

The National Trust is a registered charity, No. 205846

All rights reserved. No part of this publication may be copied, displayed, extracted, reproduced, utilised, stored in a retrieval system or transmitted in any form or by any means, electronic, mechanical or otherwise including but not limited to photocopying, recording, or scanning without the prior written permission of the publishers.

ISBN 978-1-84165-899-5

A CIP catalogue record for this book is available from the British Library.

10 9 8 7 6 5 4 3 2 1

Reproduction by Rival Colour Ltd, UK
Printed and bound by Imak, Turkey

MIX
Paper from responsible sources
FSC® C111584
www.fsc.org

This book can be ordered direct from the publisher at
www.pavilionbooks.com
Also available at www.nationaltrustbooks.co.uk